Table of Contents

Introduction

Many people have issues with being able to keep their homes organized and cleaned the way that they would like. They have formed an emotional attachment to many of the items that are present in their homes and rather than being able to let these items go, they hold on to them and let them clutter up their lives. This guidebook is meant to discuss some of the issues that cause clutter and offer many great tips for organizing each and every room in your home.

Chapter 1 starts off this guidebook with explaining why people keep items that they do not need. It discusses the emotional and guilt feelings that many people have when trying to determine whether to keep an item or get rid of it. Chapter 2 talks about some of the myths that surround clutter and how you will be able to get through them in order to achieve the organization that you desire.

The rest of the chapters found in this guidebook focus on how to organize the different rooms that are available in your home. Chapter 3 talks about organizing your living room while chapter 4 talks about the kitchen and chapter 5 talks about organizing your bathroom.

Chapter 6 continues on with how to organize your bedroom and chapter 7 gives you some great tips on keeping your closet organized as well.

Chapter 8 and 9 discuss other areas in your home that can often hold a lot of clutter and need to be organized as well. Chapter 8 gives you some hints on how to organize your office so that you can get more work done during the day while chapter 9 hits on the other storage areas in your home such as storage spaces, basements, and attics. Chapter 10 ends this guidebook by giving you some helpful hints on how to keep up your organization so that it lasts for the long term.

Chapter 1 –Why We keep Stuff

Organization is a problem that many Americans currently deal with. They are used to buying and receiving a lot of different things, but many of them are not used to having to get rid of any of these things. All of this excess stuff gets in the way and makes it really difficult to keep your home and your life organized. This guidebook is meant to help you understand why people keep things, usually for emotional reasons, and how you can de-clutter your life so it you can get your life back on track.

There are two main beliefs of why people keep the items that they have, even if they do not need the items. These two reasons are monetary attachment and emotional attachment. To start with will be the emotional issues. There are many excuses that you can hear if someone has an emotional attachment to an item including:

- *"It's been in family for years."* If someone that you were really close to has recently died, you may find that it is really difficult for you to get rid of some of their stuff and you may want to hold on to it, even if the things start to take over your whole house and life. While there is nothing wrong with keeping a couple of items from the deceased loved one that hold special meaning to you, it can get out of hand quickly if you start to decide that everything is important and you can't get rid of anything. If this is a reason why you are holding onto many items, it is a good time to let some of the things go. Pick out one or two items that hold special meaning to you and then just donate or get rid of everything else. This is great for you in so many ways including letting go of the death of a loved one and clearing up some space in your home.

- *"It was a gift."* Many people feel that if someone took the time and energy to purchase them a gift, that they should never get rid of the gift. If you really enjoy the gift and are using it all of the time, then this is fine. The problem comes when you receive a gift that just ends up in storage or taking up space in your closet. There is nothing wrong with getting rid of a gift that you have not used in years. The person who gave it to you will never remember and it is just taking up more space than it is worth in your home with all the clutter.

- *"It has sentimental value."* There is nothing wrong with keeping some items that have sentimental value to us. You might have many items that are in your house that others would see as useless, but have a lot of meaning to you and your family. If the item is truly something that holds some value to you, then it is fine to keep it. The problem can often occur when you think something has sentimental value when it really doesn't. When this occurs, you are just wasting space in your home and should take the time to go through the items to decide what is really important and what you can truly live without.

When you are dealing with any of these issues, it is important that you do not let guilt or shame get in the way of you deciding whether to keep the item or not. If you are truly interested in organizing your life, you need to take the time to decide if the item is providing some use to you or if it is just in the way. An easy way to think about it is this: If you have not used the item in the last six months and you cannot specifically name a date that you will use it in the future, then it is not worth keeping anymore. These kinds of items should just be thrown out to save you the headache of a cluttered house.

There has also been some research done to discuss why people are interested in keeping things that they just do not need. According to the director of the Anxiety Disorders Center at Hartford Hospital, Dr. David Tolin, many people will keep items for a long period of time because they are perfectionists.

Dr. Tolin explains, "They don't necessarily color-code their closets, but they have that perfectionistic streak that bites them when it gets too bad. They have the mentality that, 'If I can't make this decision perfectly, I won't do it at all." This is Dr. Tolins basic explanation of why people will keep things for a long time even if there is no reason for them to keep these items.

Basically, these people might not go around and have to have their whole life in perfect order, but they feel that if they are going to do something in their lives, then they need to do it right or not do it at all. When it comes to cleaning up their homes, they feel like all of the hassle and work will take too long and that they will not be able to do it all properly, so they decide not to do it at all. The result is that their homes become messy and disorganized and it just continues getting worse.

Another reason that Dr. Tolin lists for people wishing to hold onto things that they no longer need is because they have a fear that they will throw something away that they actually need or that is really important to them and that they won't be able to get it back. Dr. Tolin states that many people can think of many ways that they will be able to use a particular object in the future, especially if they are given the time, and therefor they are able to convince themselves not to get rid of the object. "The irony, however, is that in most cases, they never actually use the object in the way they thought of. They don't actually give the object to the person they thought of."

This means that instead of putting the item to good use, the person is instead keeping it in a drawer, in their storage area, or in their closets and it is never getting the use that it needs to in order to be useful. These items begin to just take over the home of the person who is keeping them and they soon have more stuff than they know what to do with. It is important that if you are going to start organizing your home and your life, you take the whole process seriously. If you have not used the item in the past 6 months or so and are not able to think of the exact date that you will use it next or take it straight over to the person who you want to give it to, then the item is just clutter and it is not helping anyone. Rather than convincing yourself that it is worth it to keep the item, just realize that you have no use for it and it is in your way, and get it out of your life.

Dr. Tolin lists one more reason that many people will hold onto items that they no longer need and it is a reason that was listed in a little bit of detail earlier in this chapter. Many people hold onto these items because they feel that there is an emotional attachment between then and the objects that are inside of their homes. According to Dr. Tolin, "We have things that remind us of people we love, or they remind us of happy times."

While it is normal to have some attachment to items that you own, there is a point where it can get out of hand and the person may need help in order to get rid of some of the items. For those who are considered hoarders of items, the attachment goes beyond normal to a point where the person has formed a personal and emotional connection to thousands of different items rather than just a couple. Once this happens, the person may need more than the right mindset in order to start getting rid of the things that are inside their homes.

Chapter 2 –Myths and Bad Habits About Clutter

Before you get started with cleaning out your home and getting rid of all clutter that is inside your home, it is important to understand some of the myths about bad habits with clutter so that you are able to avoid them in all of your organization. Here are some of the top myths about cluttering that you should try to avoid.

1. **I need to be organized**. While it is perfectly fine for you to want to start organizing your life, it should not be the first thing that you think of. Instead, you should be thinking about all of the things that you need to get rid of in your home. Once you have gotten rid of a lot of things, you will find that it is a whole lot easier to complete the organization.

2. **The more that I organize, the better off I am**. Organization is key in this whole process, but you need to make sure that you are not overdoing it. There needs to be a happy middle between having things in an area where you are easily able to find them and spending hours categorizing your library and alphabetizing all of your spices.

3. **I need to get tons of storage containers.** If you are able to organize your home the right way, you may find that you have no use for all of these storage containers and they are just a waste of money. Take the time to throw out anything that you don't need in your home before determining whether storage containers are the right idea for your home needs.

4. **I need to find someone to get all of the things I no longer need.** It is a great to think of all the people that you could be helping when you give all of the things you no longer need, but you may run into the problem of keeping these items and never actually giving them away. If you are able to give the item to the recipient right away, then do so. Otherwise choose to dump out your unused items or run them straight over to a thrift store when you are done organizing.

5. **I have to make sure I keep everything I might need someday.** This is a trap that many people will fall into when they are trying to organize. They worry that the second that they get rid of something, they will find that they are in need of it. For the most part, you are probably not going to use a big thing of rubber bands or some old jars that are just gathering dust. Get rid of these things and get new ones if you every actually need

them someday.

6. **Someday I will get this fixed.** How likely is it that you will actually fix that tool or product that has been sitting around broken for the past year? It is probably not all that likely. So instead of letting it sit around your house and cause a lot of clutter, throw it out while you are organizing.

7. **Once I lose weight, I'll wear these clothes.** Losing weight is an admirable goal to have, but using it as an excuse to keep the clutter in your home is not a good idea. Rather than keeping your old clothes, treat yourself to the idea that you will get to go out and purchase some new clothes once you have been able to reach your weight loss goals.

8. **I need this for a memory.** There is nothing wrong with keeping a few mementos of your past, but you need to make sure that it does not get out of hand. For example, if you have been out of high school for more than 20 years, it probably does not make much sense to have a whole bunch of t-shirts from that time, especially if you do not fit in them still. Pick one or two of your favorites and toss out the rest. Choose your mementos carefully and make sure that they do not take up too much space in your home.

9. **I must keep this because it would hurt someone's feelings.** It is more than likely that the person who gave you the gift will not even remember it in a few years and would not want you to keep the gift if you were not using it or did not want it. It is perfectly fine for you to give it to someone else who might be able to use the gift or to just get rid of it if you are not using it.

Chapter 3 –Organizing the Living Room

When you are ready to start organizing your home, the first place that you should start is the living room. Here this chapter will focus on some of the tips that you can follow in order to organize this room of your home with hardly any effort at all.

To start with, you should make a list that includes all of the activities that your family does in the living room. These things can include playing, entertaining guests, and watching television. Once you have a list, you should go through the living room and divide it up into sections so that each of these activities can occur in a different area. It is fine if the activities overlap a little if they need to.

Next, take note of which objects and furniture in the living room will be needed for each activity before taking the time to move the items where they need to go. An example of doing this includes placing some cushions and a small table over in one section so that your children can have a place to play in the room.

Now you can work on the magazines, newspapers, and books that are cluttering up the living room and separate them into two piles. One pile will be full of ones that you have read and the other will be ones that you still need to read. Make sure to recycle all of the magazines and newspapers that you do not plan to read again and then place your books onto a shelf for later or donate them if you no longer want them.

You may find that some baskets will work nice for this next tip. Take a few out in order to hold your unread newspapers, books, and magazines in and then store them either under your coffee table or other end tables. If you have your reading materials stored away, you will be able to get to them easily when you need them, but you will not have to deal with your living room having clutter all over the place.

The living room table can often be a place where a lot of random things end up at the end of the day. Take the time to clear this off in order to give your living room a cleaner look. Place your remote controls into the baskets with the reading materials, place the bills in the office, and pick up anything else that you are able to.

Make sure not to leave movies and CD's all over the place in your living room. Instead, place all of them into their cases and organize them in a rack or in your entertainment system. You can organize the movies by genre if you would like or just place them away nicely so that you are able to see the titles and pick out the one that you want when you are ready for it.

If you have your children play in your living room, it is a good idea to find a storage container that can hold all of their different toys. This can really help to cut down on all of the clutter that might be found all over your floor. Make sure to keep the box in a designated corner or area so that it is not in the way.

It is always a good idea to have a few collectible items around your living room in order to help give it a homey feeling. Make sure to not overdo it though and just pick a couple of items before either getting rid of the rest or placing them into storage.

Instead of placing picture frames on your end tables and coffee table, place them out of the way on shelves that you have or on your mantle. An even better idea is to hang them up on the wall in order to get them completely out of the way. This is a great way to get rid of all the clutter that is on your coffee table.

Try out a few of these suggestions in your living room and you will soon be amazed at how easy it is to keep your living room clean, organized, and devoid of all sorts of clutter.

Chapter 4 –Organizing Your Kitchen

Once you have finished cleaning up and organizing your living room, it is time to move on to the kitchen. The kitchen can often be one of the most difficult rooms to organize because there are so many things that you can keep in this area. It is important that you take the time to organize all the items that are in your kitchen including the utensil, cooking equipment, and grocery items as well. Here are some tips that you can use in order to make organizing your kitchen easy and simple.

The first tip that you can fallow is to make sure of the vertical space that you have available in your kitchen. For example, putting up little hooks along the walls can be the perfect way to hang up some utensils or some pots and pans instead of using up the minimal cabinet space that you have. In addition, there are many other types of wall or window hangings that you can utilize around the whole kitchen that are perfect for placing many different items on and opening up your kitchen some more.

Tray trolleys and racks are a few others things that you can use in order to add more room in the cabinets that you have and even on your kitchen counters. Rather than just placing one thing on a counter, you can get a small shelf and place multiple items together in a breeze. Many people who are looking to organize their kitchens will use tray trolleys to hold various foods or spices. They are able to just spin the trolleys around and find the item that they are looking for much easier compared to trying to see the individual items inside the cabinet. Take the time to get creative about how you are able to use these shelves and trays in order to open up room in your kitchen.

Some of the other options that you can use in your kitchen include turntable organizers, wire racks, adjustable trays, and even stackable containers. The types of organizers that you need will depend on the items that you have in your kitchen along with how big or small your current kitchen is.

Chapter 5 –Organizing Your Bathroom

Now it is time to go on to organizing your bathroom. This is a room that will take some time because there are often a lot of items that must be held within your bathroom and most bathrooms are really small. Here are some of the tips that you should take in order to get your bathroom really organized and easy to use.

The first thing that you should make sure to do is go through the bathroom and decide what kinds of things that you would like to keep and which ones you no longer need. Some of the things that you can get rid of include old makeup, medications and vitamins that are past their expiration dates, and old sunscreen. You will not be able to organize your bathroom very well if you hold on to many things that you do not have any use for anymore. Get rid of anything that will never be used again.

Next, if you like to keep some magazines in your bathroom to use, then you might find it useful to hang up a magazine rack in order to keep them all organized. Pick a spot that will be out of the way and that will not use up space that you can use for something else.

Organizing equipment will be one of your best friends in the bathroom. Find a couple of small organization containers that you can place into the drawers of your bathroom in order to hold small odds and ends such as cotton swabs, safety pin, bobby pins, and hair bands. You will want everything to have its own spot so that it is easy to find them when you need them. Make sure to put everything back in its designated spot when you are done with it in order to keep the organization going.

If you travel a lot and have many different miniature bottles of items from the hotels that you frequent, it is time to decide whether you use these items or not. If it has just become a habit to pick up these items while you are out on the road and you never actually use them, then it is time to just toss them because they are taking up more room than they are worth.

Next you will need to figure out different ways to contain the clutter that is present in your bathroom. If you have young kids, you can get a mesh bag to hold all of their bath toys when they are not being used. For other items that you use frequently in your bathroom, such as gels, body washes, conditioners, and shampoos, you can get a caddy that will stick to the wall of your shower or somewhere else that is out of the way. This way, you can keep all of the items that you need out of the way.

If you have a cabinet that is under your sink, you are sure to know how messy it can get. Many families just throw a ton of stuff under this cabinet in order to get it out of the way when they are trying to clean up the bathroom. Now is a good time to try and organize this cabinet. Take inventory of the cabinet and get rid of anything that you do not need. With everything else that is leftover, get another storage container or two that you can place all the items that you need in your bathroom.

Instead of waiting for your bathroom to get all dirty and cluttered up again before you decide to clean it again, you can make it a priority to clean it up a little every day. While this might seem like a hassle at first, doing this little thing can save you a lot of time compared to spending all day cleaning the bathroom. You may find that it is helpful to keep some cleaning supplies and disinfectant wipes under the sink so that you are able to clean up after you have cleared off your counters.

One thing that can save a lot of clutter in your bathroom is purchasing accessories like straight irons, hot curlers, and blow dryers that have cords that can be retracted. If this is not possible, you should take the time to wrap the cords up as nicely as possible so that the cords will stay out of the way while you are putting things away.

If your bathroom does not have towel racks available, it might be a good idea for you to install a few of them to hang extra towels for guests who come and visit. These towel racks are much better than leaving your towels on the ground.

Chapter 6 –Organizing Your Bedroom

You will spend a lot of time in your bedroom getting ready for work and other events, sleeping, and just relaxing. It is important that you take the time to organize your bedroom correctly so that you are able to relax and feel more comfortable in this important room. Here are some of the tips that you can follow in order to properly organize your bedroom and get it looking as nice as possible.

The first thing that you can do is get some hanging organizers for your closet. These kinds of organizers are a great way to save space in your bedroom while also making sure that important items are keeps off the floor, which can be a huge thing when you are trying to keep your room organized and neat. When you are looking for a hanging organizer, make sure to pick one that has a lot of pouches and pockets and is compact in order to hold many common bedroom items such as sunglasses, jewelry, and other hair accessories.

These kinds of organizers are perfect if you do not have very much space in your bedroom because you can fill it up and then place it into our closet without wasting hardly any of the space that you need for other things. It is also perfect if you travel around a lot because you can just take the hanging organizer and fold it up into a bag.

The next thing that you can get in order to organize your bedroom is find storage bins that can fit under your bed. There is a lot of unused space that is available under your bed that can be used to get some things out of the way. If you pick out the right kinds of storage containers, you will be able to hold a ton of stuff and find that organization is a whole lot easier.

Some of the things that you could store under bed using these bins include books, clothes that are out of season, and anything else that is just in the way and that you do not need right away. Using the storage bins that can go under your bed are perfect because everything will be out of your way, but you will be able to pull them out in no time if you are in need of the items again.

Depending on how much room you have beneath your bed, you may be able to fit at least two or three of these bins there. This is the perfect idea rather than just leaving the stuff lying around your bedroom and getting into your way. You are not using that space under your bed anyway.

If your bedroom has a desk, you might find a desktop organizer very helpful.

You can use these organizers in order to keep all of your school and work supplies in order and nice and neat. These organizers can keep your papers in order and allow your pens and pencils to have a special spot rather than rolling all over the place.

Another way that you are able to organize your bedroom is to set up some shelves that have bins. These are perfect for organizing when you are really limited on the amount of space that it available and they can fit either in your closet or in a corner to take up even less room. You are able to place pretty much any item in these storage bins that you want, but pillowcases and sheets often fit well in them. Other things that you can place in these storage bins include shoes, hats, scarves, slippers, and books. It is easy to place these items in these bins and you can get the items back out whenever you need them

When you are organizing your bedroom, it is important to take the time to organize all of the little things that you have because it will make a huge difference. While it might seem like it is a waste of time, it is a good idea to take the time to find a place for everything. You will save time in the long run because you will not have to spend as much time looking for things later. When you are not spending a ton of time looking for items in your bedroom, you can spend that time doing other important things.

Chapter 7 –Organizing Your Closet

While you are working on organizing your bedroom, you can work on organizing your closet at the same time. There are a lot of closets that seem to just catch random items that are in the way and that we want to clean up. This will lead to a closet that is way over cluttered and difficult to find things in. After you are done cleaning up your bedroom and getting it easier to find things in, you can follow some of these tips in order to clean out and organize your closet at the same time.

The first thing that you need to do is simplify your closet. This means that you need to get rid of as many of the clothes, shoes, and other accessories that you are able to. A good rule of thumb is that if you have not worn the article of clothing in a year or more, then you should either sell it or donate it. It does not matter how nice the article of clothing looks or how much you think that you like it. If you have not worn it, then obviously you do not like it as much as you thought you did. Not only is this a great way to clear out your closet, it can help you to make a little extra money in the process.

After you have gone through your closet and gotten rid of the items that you no longer need, you should take the time to color coordinate your closet. While this may seem like you are overdoing it a little bit, it is a great way for you to save time when you are getting ready for work or school in the morning. Instead of searching through your closet in the hopes of finding the right pair of pants and right shirt to go together, you can just look in the color that you want and it should be right there for you.

Hang up as much of your clothes and other accessories as possible. If you fold up all of your clothes in your closet, it is soon going to become a mess because you will be in a hurry when searching around for something and everything will become a mess. Get some nice padded or wooden hangers that will be gentle on your clothes rather than using old wire hangers. For your pants or skirts, you may want to consider using hangers that have clips on them so that these items stay nice and wrinkle free until the next time that you are ready to wear them.

Once you have gotten all of your clothes hung up nicely and color coordinated in your closet, it is time to organize the other things that are in the way. one of the best things that you can do is invest in some organizing containers in order to keep everything in one place that is easy to find. You could get a storage container to hold your leggings and tights and another to hold your extra jewelry. A nice wall hanging might be nice to hold your shoes so that they are not lying all over the floor the next time that you need them.

While you are organizing your closet, make sure to take the time to keep as much of your belongings at eye level. Many people will forget about items that they keep on high shelving where it cannot be seen easily. If you are forgetting about items, then they are just taking up space and should be thrown out instead. This does not mean that you cannot use the shelves and other storage opportunities that are higher up. Just make sure to use them wisely. One idea that you may want to consider is placing your out of season clothing and accessories up there until you have a need of them. Anything that you plan to use on a regular basis should be kept at eye level so that you can have easy access to it.

You should always make sure to keep track of some of your favorite items that are stored in your closet. This can be really important if you are one of those people who have a really difficult time trying to decide what you should wear in the morning. If this sounds like you, take the time to group together outfits ahead of time and then hang them up so they are easy for you to get to. This can save you a ton of time when you are trying to get ready for a special event or you do not have time to decide what to wear in the morning.

Finally, hooks should become your best friend in your closet. These inexpensive items can be hung up anywhere inside your closet and can hold so many things, such as coats, sweaters, necklaces, hats, and belts. Put up a few of these hooks to hold onto extra items that you do not have a place for.

Chapter 8—Organizing Your Office

If you are feeling really ambitious after cleaning up and organizing the majority of your home, you may be interested in trying to tackle your own office. It does not matter if your office is within your home or in a separate building, your life can be much simpler if you take the time to organize it.

To start organizing your office, you need to take the time to evaluate the space that you have. There are four areas within your office that you should analyze before getting started and these include:

- **Desk placement**-where is your desk located within the office? If you have your desk facing the door, it might be a good idea to consider moving it to a back corner and turn it so that it looks towards a wall. If you have the desk facing the opposite direction of the door, you will find it much easier to focus on your work and others who are passing by will be much less likely to stop in to bother you.

- **Desk space**-you should take the time to determine if the desk that you have is meeting your current needs. Are you able to keep all of the things on your desk that you need while still getting work done? If not, then it is a good idea to consider getting a table that you can place next to your desk to add on the extra room that is needed.

- **Desktop items**- how many of the items on your desk are used for work and how many are more personal items such as mugs, plaques, and pictures. If the majority of the items on your desk are of a personal nature, it is best if you cut them down a little bit. It is fine to have a couple of these items, but they should not be taking up the majority of your desk. If you would like to keep these items in your office, make sure to add on a shelf to place these items.

- **Computer and other devices**-take a look at all of the work related technology that is present on your desk and determine if it is located in an area where they are easy to use. If they are not, you will need to take the time to move them to better meet your needs for working.

Now that you have taken the time to evaluate the space that you have, you can get to work organizing your office. The first thing that you should do is deal with the paper that is present in your office as this is likely to be the issue that is causing the most clutter. To do this, you should take the time to look over each piece of paper that is in your office and sort it into one of the following categories:

- **Toss it**: if you no longer need the piece of paper, then it makes sense that you should get rid of it.

- **Action required**: if the paper will need you to make a decision about it, you can place it into a pile for later. This is not the time to make the decision since you are spending your time organizing. After you are done organizing, you can look over the paper and make the required decisions.

- **Review**: there are some documents that you might need to review more later once you have more time. Put papers such as these in their own pile.

- **File**: if a document holds important information that needs to be used for reference or historical purposes, but does not need to you perform action on it, then it should go into this pile.

- **Awaiting response**: these kinds of documents will include ones where you have delegated a task to another worker or which had a question that you are waiting on an answer for should go into this pile.

- **Projects**: any documents that have to do with a project that you are currently working on should go in this pile. You can also take the time to split these up by project if you are working on more than one at a time.

After you have taken the time to go through all of the paper that is cluttering up your office, it is time to bring in all of the storage containers that are necessary in order to organize the rest of your office. Some of the things that you will need to do this process include binders, baskets, and bins.

To start with, you can get out some binders and label them based on the current projects that you are working on. If you would like to, you can also take the time to color code them so that you can easily keep everything separated and find it when you need it. Any documents that you already have and any that come in later that have to do with a particular project should be placed into the correct binder for proper organization and to make it easier for you to find the information later on.

Next, you can create bins for all of the categories that were listed above for the papers that you receive in the future. Place all of the papers that you already have into these categories so that you can go through them when you have more time. In addition, keep these bins so that when new papers come in you can easily sort them out so they go where they belong right away.

Once these bins are in place, you will have to make sure to take the time and go through them a few times a week. In your schedule, make sure to set aside about 30 minutes a few times a week to do this process. Review all of the documents that you have and take the actions that are necessary to get everything done. When you do this step properly, you make sure that all of the paperwork stays organized and that it doesn't get to a point where it will all be overwhelming when you get to it.

If you have a computer, it can save you a lot of time and hassle to give up paper and choose to store your documents electronically. Ask your boss and coworkers if they would be willing and able to send all communications to you through email so that everything can stay on your computer and you do not have to worry about excess paper getting in the way. When you use the electronic form of communication, it is much easier to find papers, file them, and reference them when needed in the future. You can also take the time to scan original documents so that you have an electronic form of it available as well.

Notepads can often become your best friend when you are trying to organize your office. You should make sure to keep a couple of them around for each of the tasks that you have to take care of. Label them using the project name so that you know instantly what the notes are for.

You can use these notepads to write down anything about the project that comes up. Some of these things include messages that you get, ideas that come up concerning the project, meetings, and even important dates and people. Using the notepads can help to keep everything in one place so that you are not wasting a lot of time trying to find your notes or keep track of important things.

Chapter 9 –Organizing Your Storage Spaces, Basement, and Attics

This next chapter is going to discuss organizing the other areas that are left over in your home, namely, the attics, basement, and storage spaces. These are areas in the home that often catch whatever you cannot fit anywhere else so they will probably take you the most time in order to properly organize.

To start out with organizing these areas, you will need to take the time and go through all of the items and decide what you really want to keep and what you can easily live without. You are sure to have many items in these areas of your home that you have forgotten about over the years and that does not have any purpose anymore. Take the time to get rid of all the things that you have not used in years and that do not have any purpose anymore. You might be surprised at how much more room you have leftover in these areas and how much the organizing work will be cut down.

Once you are done with sorting out which things that you want to keep and what you are going to throw away, there are a few steps that you can take in order to organize the items that you still have leftover. You need to determine out of the items that are left, which ones you are likely to use often and which ones you just need every once in a while. For example, if you are storing cleaning supplies in a storage closet, you will want those placed up front so that you can get to them easily while things like Christmas decorations will be fine further in the back of the storage area.

You should also take the time to think vertically when it comes to your storage areas. If there is any shelving available, take complete advantage of it and place as many things as you can in an organized manner. If the area does not have any shelving, you may want to consider putting some into the area. This is a really easy way to get things out of the way and to have some organization in an area that is usually really messy. Having these shelves is a great way to group items that are similar together and makes it easier for you to see the things that are in the storage area.

Next, you will have to think about the elements with some of your items, especially in the case of storing things into your basements and attics. If you have a lot of valuables that you are keeping in the basement, you need to make sure to keep them off the floor so that they do not become susceptible to water damage. Items that are stored in the attic will have to deal with extreme changes in temperatures so be careful what kinds of things that you are storing in this area.

Clear containers should become your best friend in these storage areas. You can place a ton of things in these bins and can easily see what is in each of them with very little effort. Be careful of how big of bins that you get. While it might seem like a good idea to get a huge bin to hold a lot of things, it will soon get too heavy to move around. Pick smaller bins that can fit a couple of things in them for easy maneuvering and ease of access.

One thing that you should keep in mind when you are organizing the storage areas in your home is that you should not need to find a flashlight to figure out where things are. If you are using a flashlight every time that you go into one of these storage areas, then you have not correctly organized the area. Add in some lights to these areas and place items in an organized manner so that when you go into the storage area, you are able to see what everything is at a glance without a flashlight.

Make labeling a priority when you are organizing these storage areas in your home. No matter what you think, you will never remember what you placed in each bin a couple of months down the road. Make lists or use a labeler to mark what is in each of the bins as you go through the process.

You will also want to take the time to make organizing these storage areas a priority so that they do not become messy and disorganized again. It is good to do this at least a couple of times a year. Often, it can be easy to throw extra items in these storage areas and you will soon have a complete mess again. Taking some time a few times each year will make the task more manageable and helps you to be able to keep track of everything that you are keeping in your storage area.

Chapter 10 –Maintaining Your Organization

After you have taken the time to follow some of the tips that were listed in this guidebook on how to organize your home, it is time to figure out ways that you will keep up the organization rather than falling back into your old patterns and having your home be a complete mess a couple of months later. This chapter is devoted to giving you some easy tips that you can follow in order to maintain your organization for the long term.

To start with, you need to make sure that the process of organization makes you feel good. When you feel good about all of the effort that you are putting in while organizing, you will be much more likely to continue doing so in the future. In addition, once you have taken the time to find a place for all of the items in your home, it is critical that you do so every day. Once you are done using an item, put it away immediately in order to avoid clutter. Some more tips about what you can do to maintain organization in your home include:

1. **Regular maintenance:** instead of waiting for your home to become a complete mess and having to spend hours cleaning it up, take a few minutes every day in order to do a quick cleaning.

2. **Be aware:** when you are doing your few minutes of picking up each day, take the time to think of what types of organization are working and which ones you do not like. You should write down a list of these things so that you can utilize them the next time you do a complete organization of your home.

3. **Re-organize:** No matter how much work you put into organizing your home each day, there will come a time when the clutter will start to come back. If this seems to be happening often, you might need to take the time to figure out a new way of organizing that will work out better for your needs.

4. **If it is working, don't waste time on it:** it does not make sense to spend a lot of time trying to fix systems that are working fine for you. Only fix the organization systems that are causing you some issues.

5. **Appreciate the work you are doing:** you have put a lot of time into your home and it is important for you to take the time to appreciate it. When you love the environment that you are in, you will want to take care of it much better.

6. **Have a reward for keeping your home organized:** when you

turn the process of organization into a chore, you are much less likely
to keep on doing it. Instead, turn it into a game that you will enjoy and
add in a reward to it and you will be more likely to keep on organizing.

There are many other things that you can keep in mind when you are trying to
keep your home organized. First off, remember that not everything has to go
perfectly when you are organizing for the first time. Figure out a system that
works out the best for you right now and if it ends up not working at some
point, you can always change it up.

Just because you do not have a lot of money in order to organize your home
does not mean that you cannot figure out some great ways to keep up
organization. Creativity is one of the best things that you can learn how to
utilize if you are on a short budget.

You can also realize that spending a little bit of money on organizing your
home is a good investment in the long run. Some organization containers
such as key racks, shelf racks, and other containers will often pay for
themselves in terms of convenience after a couple of months. If you are really
worried about money, you will be able to use some of the containers or other
things around your home rather than purchasing new items.

The important thing that you have to remember about organization is that you
must do it in a way that works the best for you. A method that works for
someone else may work out horribly for you. Just remember to start out the
organization of any room by going through and getting rid of anything that
you will no longer use. This will save you a lot of time and effort when you
are ready to organize the rest of the room.

Chapter 11-Conclusion

Organization can have so many benefits for your life and can make it much easier for you to find the things that you need in your own home. Rather than wasting a lot of time sorting through the clutter of things that you do not need any more each day, take the time to organize your life and see how much better things can get.

Hopefully this guidebook was able to provide you with some great tips that you can use in organizing any room in your house. The first step to achieving the organization that you want is to just get up and get started!

Work Cited

http://homeorganizationtipsonestep.blogspot.com/2008/05/why-do-we-keep-all-that-stuff.html

http://www.oprah.com/home/Why-People-Become-Compulsive-Hoarders

http://gretchenrubin.com/happiness_project/2012/01/9-common-myths-about-decluttering/

http://www.ehow.com/how_2121457_organize-living-room.html

http://ezinearticles.com/?Tips-to-Organize-Your-Kitchen&id=5073341

http://www.sheknows.com/home-and-gardening/articles/810958/10-tips-to-organize-your-bathroom

http://www.squidoo.com/how-to-organize-your-bedroom

http://www.howdoesshe.com/6-tips-for-organizing-your-closet/

http://workingmoms.about.com/od/yourcareer/a/5-Tips-to-Organize-Your-Office.htm

http://www.daily-journal.com/life/home_garden/tips-for-organizing-attics-and-basements/article_4cb46d77-ccf4-5fd2-a914-64f2099248d9.html

http://www.wikihow.com/Maintain-Home-Organization